Developing a Nation

Developing a Nation

Student Objectives

I will be able to:

- **Read and analyze personal journals, diaries, and informational texts about the past.**

- **Share ideas with my peers.**

- **Build my vocabulary knowledge.**

- **Write informational, narrative, and opinion texts.**

Credits
Editor: Joanne Tangorra
Contributing Editors: Jeffrey B. Fuerst, Brett Kelly
Creative Director: Laurie Berger
Art Directors: Melody DeJesus, Kathryn DelVecchio-Kempa, Doug McGredy, Chris Moroch
Production: Kosta Triantafillis
Director of Photography: Doug Schneider
Photo Assistant: Jackie Friedman

Photo credits: Cover, Back Cover: © nik wheeler / Alamy; Table of Contents C, Page 22A: "Lewis and Clark at Three Forks" by Edgar S. Paxon, Oil on Canvas, 1912, Montana Historical Society, Montana State Capitol Art Collection, X1912.07.01, Don Beatty Photographer 10/1999; Page 2, 22C: Crossing the Ford, Platte River, Colorado (oil on canvas), Whittredge, Thomas Worthington (1820-1910) / Century Association, New York, USA / Bridgeman Images; Page 3A: National Park Service/U.S. Department of the Interior; Page 3B, 13: © ClassicStock / Alamy; Page 4B: Black 1914 Model T Ford (USA), side view / Dorling Kindersley/UIG / Bridgeman Images; Page 6, 17A, 24B: The Granger Collection, NYC; Page 8B: © Heritage Image Partnership Ltd / Alamy; Page 15: National Park Service; Page 16: © Everett Collection Historical / Alamy; Page 17B: Train Passengers on the Kansas Pacific Railroad, shooting buffalo for sport in the 1870's (colour litho), American School, (19th century) / Private Collection / Peter Newark Western Americana / Bridgeman Images; Page 18: © North Wind Picture Archives / Alamy; Page 22B: The Louisiana Purchase of 1803 (colour litho), American School, (20th century) / Private Collection / Peter Newark American Pictures / Bridgeman Images; Page 24: Whitman Mission National Historic Site; Page 25A: © Corbis; Page 26: Dr John McLoughlin at Fort Vancouver welcoming Narcissa Whitman and Eliza Spalding, the first American woman to cross the Great Plains to Oregon in 1836, 1938 (litho), Schwarz, F.H. (1894-1951) & Faulkner, B. (1881-1966) (after) / Private Collection / Peter Newark American Pictures / Bridgeman Images/Oregon State Archives, Oregon Secretary of State, OSS #0025; Page 27: Joan Helm Jensen Collection/Oregon Historical Society/#bb011799; Page 28A: Gold prospectors using a 'long tom' sluice at Spanish Flat, California, 1852 (b/w photo), American Photographer, (19th century) / Private Collection / Peter Newark American Pictures / Bridgeman Images

Permissions: Dust Bowl Refugee words and music by Woody Guthrie, WGP/TRO, © copyright 1960 (Renewed), 1963 (Renewed) Woody Guthrie Publications, Inc. & Ludlow Music, Inc., New York, NY administered by Ludlow Music, Inc. Used by permission.

ISBN: 978-1-4900-9203-4 **B**

Tips for Text Annotation

As you read closely for different purposes, remember to annotate the text. Use the symbols below. Add new symbols in the spaces provided.

Symbol	Purpose
underline	Identify a key detail.
⭐	Star an important idea in the margin.
① ② ③	Mark a sequence of events.
(magma)	Circle a key word or phrase.
?	Mark a question you have about information in the text. Write your question in the margin.
!	Indicate an idea in the text you find interesting. Comment on this idea in the margin.

Your annotations might look like this.

The Gold Rush

Notes

16   The migration on the Oregon Trail became ① an annual event. Thousands of emigrants began ② to join the wagon trains heading West. Then in ⭐ 1848, gold was discovered in California. The (lure) of rich farmlands now changed to fields of gold. ③ By 1850, more than fifty thousand people traveled the Oregon Trail West. <u>Instead of turning toward Oregon near the end of the trail, many turned to California.</u> They hoped to find their fortune mining or panning for gold instead of farming.

That's a lot of people!

Who was the first person to discover gold?

LEXILE® is a trademark of MetaMetrics, Inc., and is registered in the United States and abroad.

E-book and digital teacher's guide available at benchmarkuniverse.com.

BENCHMARK EDUCATION COMPANY
145 Huguenot Street • New Rochelle, NY • 10801

Toll-Free 1-877-236-2465
www.benchmarkeducation.com
www.benchmarkuniverse.com

Table of Contents

How do communities evolve?

Notes

The Open Road

ROUT 66

by Monica Halpern

1   The first automobiles appeared in the 1890s. Powered by an electric motor instead of horses, they were called "horseless carriages." At that time, there were only 144 miles of paved roads in the nation. When people went for a drive, cars bounced along dirt tracks. Dust blew into their eyes, and mud splattered their clothes.

2   Not only were there few paved roads in those days, but there were no gas stations or road maps. The new motorcars broke down often. For this reason, people did not go far. The first cars were also extremely expensive. Few people could afford them, so there was little reason for the country to build interstate highways. For many, horse-drawn carriages or trains were still the best way to travel.

"People can have the Model T in any color they want—so long as it's black." —Henry Ford

3   Then in 1908, Henry Ford introduced the Model T automobile. Unlike those before it, this car was affordable. Because it didn't cost much, many people bought it. As more people owned cars, the need for paved roads, gas stations, and new maps increased. As a result, the Model T helped change transportation.

FROM ROADS TO HIGHWAYS

1908: Model Ts are mass produced.

1916: Congress passes the Federal-Aid Road Act.

1926: Route 66 is commissioned.

4   People with cars wanted to go places. They wanted to hit the open road and explore America. However, to do so they needed better roads. So in 1916 Congress passed the Federal-Aid Road Act. It made funds available to help states build two-lane interstate highways. Workers would build the new roads, creating new jobs.

5   Route 66 was one of the first good roads. In the 1920s it linked small towns and big cities from Chicago to Los Angeles. It stretched about 3,850 kilometers (2,400 miles) across two-thirds of the country. Local merchants built gas stations, motels, and all-night diners beside the highway. Some built special attractions for tourists. People came to see the sights. Others drove west to California seeking a better life. By the 1930s, truckers began transporting goods cross-country on Route 66. Many of these travelers bought gas and food and stayed in the motels along the highway. Route 66 became the perfect open road.

6   Today not much is left of Route 66. Other highways are bigger and faster. But travelers can still find road signs that show where America's oldest highway once stretched.

1937:
Route 66 is
finished.

1956:
Federal-Aid Highway Act of
1956 establishes national
Interstate Highway System.

1982:
Interstate
Highway System
is completed.

Notes

Dust Bowl Refugees

1   Beginning in 1931, the Great Plains region began suffering from drought. After months without rain, soil that used to be fertile became arid and barren. Crops that were once lush soon wilted and died. Then heavy winds caused a series of dust storms to ravage the Midwest.

2   In 1933 alone there were around thirty-eight documented dust storms, or black blizzards. By 1934, the area seemed like a desert. Then on April 14, 1935, Black Sunday happened. Winds began to blow and the worst black blizzard hit. Skies filled with dust. Houses were buried under mounds of sediment. Families tied rope to each other as they tried to make it from their barns to their houses.

The storms were like blizzards, covering everything in their path with dust.

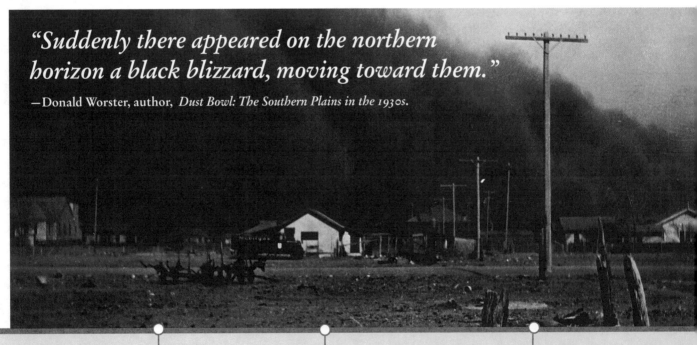

"Suddenly there appeared on the northern horizon a black blizzard, moving toward them."
—Donald Worster, author, *Dust Bowl: The Southern Plains in the 1930s.*

DUST BOWL TIME LINE

1931:
Drought hits the Plains; crops die; dust storms begin.

1933 :
Number of dust storms increases to 38 in the year.

1934:
Dust storms spread, affecting 27 states.

a family relocating to California

"The land just blew away; we had to go somewhere."

—Kansas preacher, June 1936

3   Finally, when the blizzard stopped, more than 400,000 people had lost their homes and farms. These "dust bowl refugees"—many of them from the hard-hit state of Oklahoma—had no choice but to flee the Great Plains and relocate. They packed their cars with whatever they could carry and left their old lives behind. Many hit the road and migrated to the Northwest, emigrating to California, Washington, or Oregon. They hoped the open roads would lead to a better life.

1935:
On April 14, Black Sunday, the worst black blizzard occurs.

1938:
Replowing of land, tree planting, and other conservation methods begin; drought continues.

1939:
Rain comes in the fall, finally ending the drought.

Woody Guthrie (1912–1967)

4   Woody Guthrie was an American singer and songwriter. Like others from Oklahoma, when the dust bowl hit, Guthrie took to the road. He traveled Route 66 seeking work in order to support his family. He became one of the  many "dust bowl refugees." Guthrie wrote about his experiences on the road. Guthrie's songs tell of life on the road and the hope for better times.

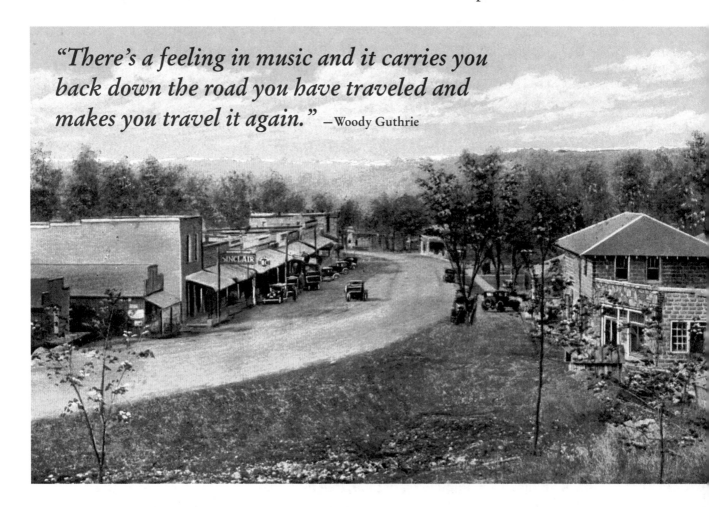

"There's a feeling in music and it carries you back down the road you have traveled and makes you travel it again." —Woody Guthrie

"Dust Bowl Refugee"

music and lyrics by Woody Guthrie

1   I'm a dust bowl refugee,
Just a dust bowl refugee,
From that dust bowl to the peach bowl,
Now that peach fuzz is a-killin' me.

5   'Cross the mountains to the sea,
Come the wife and kids and me.
It's a hot old dusty highway
For a dust bowl refugee.

Hard, it's always been that way,
10 Here today and on our way
Down that mountain, 'cross the desert,
Just a dust bowl refugee.

We are ramblers, so they say,
We are only here today,
15 Then we travel with the seasons,
We're the dust bowl refugees.

From the south land and the drought land,
Come the wife and kids and me,
And this old world is a hard world
20 For a dust bowl refugee.

Yes, we ramble and we roam
And the highway that's our home,
It's a never-ending highway
For a dust bowl refugee.

25 Yes, we wander and we work
In your crops and in your fruit,
Like the whirlwinds on the desert
That's the dust bowl refugees.

I'm a dust bowl refugee,
30 I'm a dust bowl refugee,
And I wonder will I always
Be a dust bowl refugee?

9

Black Sunday: An Eyewitness Account

1   April 14, 1935, is the date of the worst dust storm in our nation's history, now known as Black Sunday. Pauline Winkler Grey, who lived with her husband in Meade County, Kansas, gives this first person account of what happened that day.

2   "By noon the radio gave warning that the barometer was falling rapidly; this was almost a sure sign that there would be a dust storm soon. . . .

3   "I rushed to the window. . . . On the south there was blue sky, golden sunlight and tranquility; on the north, there was a menacing curtain of boiling black dust. . . . It had the appearance of a mammoth waterfall in reverse—color as well as form. As the wall of dust and sand struck our house the sun was instantly blotted out completely. Gravel particles clattered against the windows and pounded down on the roof. We stood in our living room in pitch blackness. . . . Finally, we groped our way to the wall switch and turned on the light. . . . "

4   "When we flipped the switch again, we could see only a dark brown mass of soil pressed tightly against the outside of the glass. . . . Sometime before normal sunset time, the sun reappeared briefly. . . . The wind gradually subsided . . . but fine particles of wheat-land soil sifted down from the sky. . . . "

5   Pauline Winkler Grey and her husband were more fortunate than many others. Their home wasn't destroyed. Most important of all, they survived.

BuildReflectWrite

Build Knowledge

Identify some cause-and-effect relationships discussed in the selections you read this week, and explain in a few sentences why they were important in the nation's development.

	"The Open Road"	"Dust Bowl Refugees"
Cause		
Effect		
Importance:		

Reflect

How do communities evolve?

Based on this week's texts, write down new ideas and questions you have about the essential question.

_____

_____

_____

_____

_____

_____

Writing to Sources

Narrative

Using facts and details you learned from "The Open Road," "Dust Bowl Refugees," and "Black Sunday," write a letter from the point of view of a "dust bowl refugee" traveling west in the 1930s.

Remember to annotate as you read.

Building the Transcontinental Railroad by Andrea Matthews

Notes

1   In 1830 the first railroad in the United States opened in Baltimore, and it had just 21 kilometers (13 miles) of track. Other railroad lines were built, mostly in the Northeast. Soon the East Coast was crisscrossed with train tracks, connecting cities.

2   By the 1850s, railroads were changing cities. For example, in 1850 Chicago had 30,000 people and one railroad. By 1856 the city had ten railroads, and by 1860 its population had tripled due to the rail system. The railroads affected everyday life and how people did business.

3   Farmers shipped corn and wheat through Chicago by rail. Factories were built, and their products were shipped to customers via the railroad. Hotels sprang up for visiting business travelers. New housing was built for the additional workers. Suburbs grew up around areas where people used the railroads to commute to work.

The first American steam locomotive, called the Tom Thumb, traveled at the speed of just 29 kilometers (18 miles) per hour.

Notes

4   A few dreamers wanted to expand the railroad to the lightly settled West, but there was little demand for it. Then gold was discovered in California in 1848. Word spread and people rushed there to look for gold. They found a place that had great weather and fine soil. Soon other people moved there to farm or start businesses.

5   Travelers crossed the plains in covered wagons or sailed around South America to reach California. Either way, the trip took four months or more. People wanted a better way to travel to the West. Also, farmers and business owners in the West needed a faster way to ship their goods east. Leaders began to talk about building a transcontinental railroad. Suddenly, the dreamers' idea of joining the eastern and western coasts together began to make sense.

It is in our power to open an immense interior country to . . . unite our eastern and western shores firmly together.
—Samuel Dexter, editor of the *Western Emigrant*, in 1832

The trip across the country was slow, hard, and often dangerous.

> *"A great Railroad . . . connecting the Atlantic with the Pacific ocean . . . is the most magnificent project ever [imagined].*

—Theodore Judah, 1857

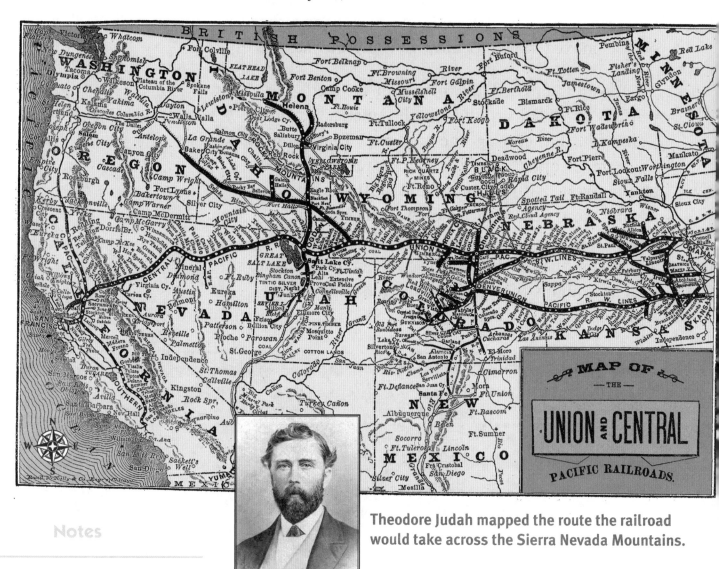

Theodore Judah mapped the route the railroad would take across the Sierra Nevada Mountains.

6   Building a railroad across the country was a huge project. It would require money, a team of engineers, armies of workers, and a leader. Theodore Judah was a young engineer who had built railroads in the East. He believed that a transcontinental railroad could and should be built.

7   Judah went to Washington, D.C. to ask the government for land and money. He convinced President Abraham Lincoln to sign the Pacific Railroad Act of 1862. This plan set up two railroad companies. The Central Pacific Railroad Company would begin in California, laying track east. The Union Pacific Railroad Company would start at the Missouri River, laying track west. They would meet somewhere in the middle.

8   Each company would receive 6,400 (later doubled to 12,800) acres of land and $48,000 in government bonds for each mile of track built. The company that got the farthest would make the most money. The land and money proved a good incentive for each company to do its best to win. The Union Pacific seemed to have the easier job. It was building across flat land. The Central Pacific had to run track through the Sierra Nevada Mountains. Either way, the race was on.

9   At first, workers were asked to lay 1.6 km (1 mile) of track per day. Then the goal became 3.2 km (2 miles) per day. One day, the Union Pacific men began work at 3 a.m. and laid more than 13 km (8 miles) of track, making the competition fierce.

10   However, the Central Pacific team refused to be beaten. They announced that a special team of workers would lay 16 km (10 miles) of track per day. The men were promised four days' pay for one day of work. By 7 p.m. they had put down their tools, as they had laid 16.1 km (10 miles and 56 feet) of track.

This marker is near Promontory, Utah.

15

11   Who were these amazing workers? Many were immigrants glad to make two to four dollars per day. There were Irish, German, Chinese, and Swedish workers. Others were former enslaved laborers or ex-soldiers. At the project's peak, more than 30,000 workers helped to construct the railroad. They built tunnels through mountains, laid rail across deserts, and dug through snowstorms, mudslides, and avalanches. Nothing stopped progress.

Chinese workers, in traditional clothing, excavated the track bed of the Central Pacific Railroad.

12   The greatest contribution came from the more than 10,000 Chinese immigrants who worked to finish the railroad. In addition to laying track, they were often trained to use explosives. They used dynamite to blast train tunnels and lay track through the mountains. This was hazardous work. The worker was lowered down the cliff in a basket. He drilled a hole in the rock, inserted explosives, and lit them. Then the worker was quickly pulled back up the cliff before the blast.

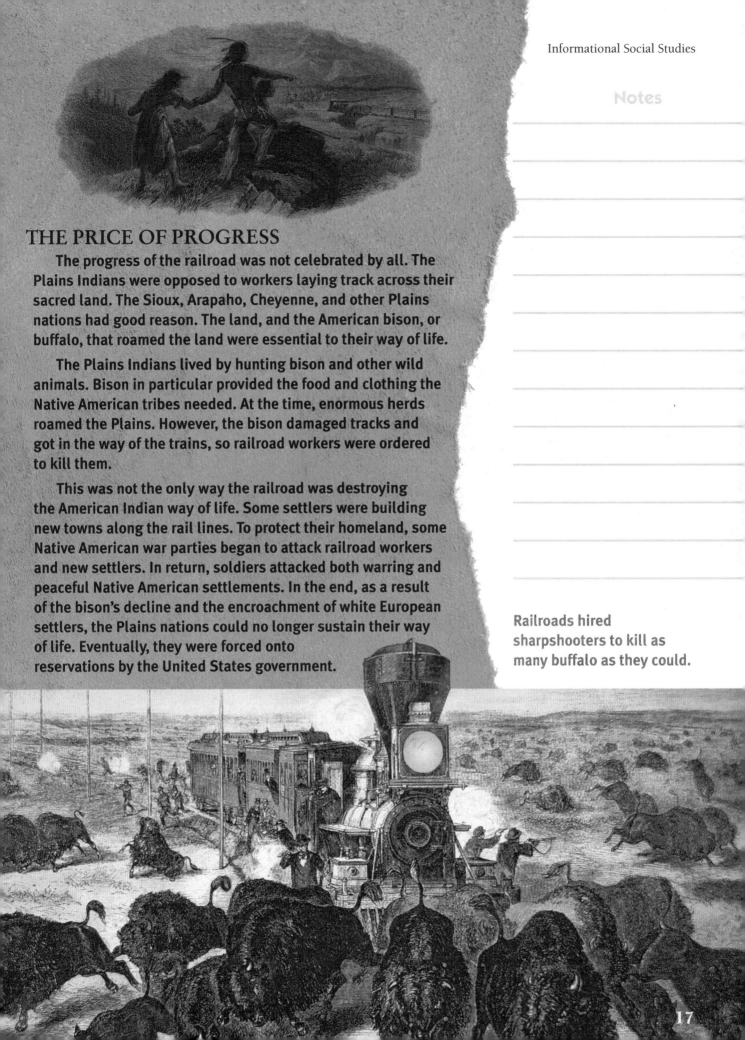

THE PRICE OF PROGRESS

The progress of the railroad was not celebrated by all. The Plains Indians were opposed to workers laying track across their sacred land. The Sioux, Arapaho, Cheyenne, and other Plains nations had good reason. The land, and the American bison, or buffalo, that roamed the land were essential to their way of life.

The Plains Indians lived by hunting bison and other wild animals. Bison in particular provided the food and clothing the Native American tribes needed. At the time, enormous herds roamed the Plains. However, the bison damaged tracks and got in the way of the trains, so railroad workers were ordered to kill them.

This was not the only way the railroad was destroying the American Indian way of life. Some settlers were building new towns along the rail lines. To protect their homeland, some Native American war parties began to attack railroad workers and new settlers. In return, soldiers attacked both warring and peaceful Native American settlements. In the end, as a result of the bison's decline and the encroachment of white European settlers, the Plains nations could no longer sustain their way of life. Eventually, they were forced onto reservations by the United States government.

Railroads hired sharpshooters to kill as many buffalo as they could.

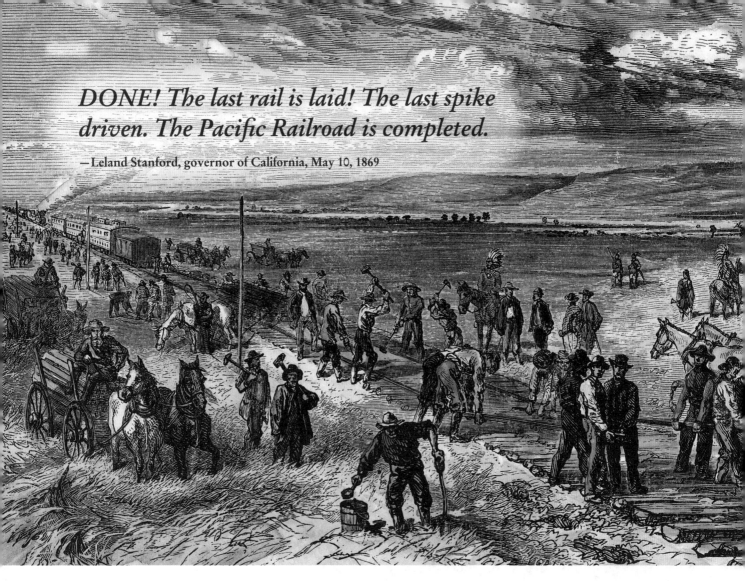

DONE! The last rail is laid! The last spike driven. The Pacific Railroad is completed.

—Leland Stanford, governor of California, May 10, 1869

13   People had expected the transcontinental railroad to be completed in 1876. Instead, it was completed in 1869, seven years early. The two railroad companies that had laid the tracks agreed to meet to lay the last rail at Promontory Point, Utah, on May 10.

14   On the big day, hundreds of people gathered. The governor of California, Leland Stanford, drove in the golden spike that joined together the Central Pacific and Union Pacific railroads. The crowd cheered while bands played.

TRANSCONTINENTAL RAILROAD TIME LINE

1830:
First steam locomotive, Tom Thumb, is built in Baltimore.

1848:
Gold is discovered in California.

1860:
Theodore Judah maps railroad route.

AMERICAN TRAVELOGUE

In his book *Roughing It* (1872), American author Mark Twain describes his 1861 trip west before the railroad was built. He traveled by mule-drawn coach from St. Joseph, Missouri, to Carson City, Nevada, in only twenty-one days.

The coach shot from the station as if . . . from a cannon. . . . It was a fierce and furious gallop . . . till we reeled off ten or twelve miles. . . . So we flew along all day [until we] landed at Fort Kearney, fifty-six hours out from St. Joe—THREE HUNDRED MILES!

Twain later describes the railroad journey he took about ten years later.

At 4:20 p.m., Sunday, we rolled out of the station of Omaha, and started westward. . . . We sped along at the rate of thirty miles an hour, . . . the fastest living we had ever experienced . . . Our train . . . rushed into the night. . . . Then to bed in luxurious couches . . . and . . . awoke the next morning . . . three hundred miles from Omaha—fifteen hours and forty minutes out.

15   Less than a week after the last rail was laid, train service began. The trip from New York to San Francisco took about a week and cost far less than the long journeys by sea or across land. It cut the price of cross-country travel from $1,000 to $150, making the trip much more affordable for the public. As a result, more settlers rode the trains west on their way to building new homes, farms, and communities.

16   The transcontinental railroad changed the nation. By linking East with West, the railroad helped unite the nation. Americans began to feel they were citizens of the United States, not just members of their local community.

1862:
President Lincoln signs the Pacific Railroad Act.

April 1869:
Workers lay a record 16 km (10 miles) of track in one day.

May 1869:
Transcontinental railroad is completed seven years early.

Word Study Read

Remember to annotate as you read.

Notes

The Pony Express

1   The Pony Express was a mail delivery service between Missouri and California. It was created to provide faster mail delivery to the West. Before then, the fastest way to transport mail was by stagecoach, which took twenty-five days.

2   A man named William Hepburn Russell came up with the idea for the new mail service. He hired around eighty young men to carry mail by horseback from St. Joseph, Missouri, to Sacramento, California. There were around 190 relay stations at 16-kilometer (10-mile) intervals where a rider changed horses before proceeding on. A rider ate and slept at home stations, spaced 80 to 160 km (50 to 100 miles) apart, after finishing his run. Then a new rider was substituted to continue the trip.

3   On April 3, 1860, the Pony Express began its first run. From the start, it was proclaimed a big success. The mail was delivered in ten days. That was great progress from twenty-five days by coach!

4   The Pony Express riders rode through blizzards and flooded rivers. Nothing interfered with delivering the mail. Stories and songs were written about their courage. Many riders became celebrities, the superstars of their day!

5   On October 24, 1861, the transcontinental telegraph lines were completed. Messages could be transmitted across the country in a few seconds. That was the end of the Pony Express, but we still remember it as one of the most exciting chapters in our history.

BuildReflectWrite

Build Knowledge

Jot down some notes about the transcontinental railroad in the chart below.

Transcontinental Railroad	
1. List three important events in the development of the transcontinental railroad.	**2. Who built the railroad?**
3. What were some positive effects of the railroad?	**4. What were some negative effects of the railroad?**

Reflect

How do communities evolve?

Based on this week's texts, write down new ideas and questions you have about the essential question.

_____

_____

_____

_____

_____

_____

_____

Writing to Sources

Informative/Explanatory

How did advancements in transportation change American society? After reading "The Open Road," "Dust Bowl Refugees," and "Building the Transcontinental Railroad," write a short essay that answers this question. Support your essay with evidence from each passage.

Notes

The Oregon Trail

1   In 1803, President Thomas Jefferson purchased the Louisiana Territory from France. The Louisiana Purchase doubled the size of the United States, opening up the West for settlers. First, the region had to be mapped. So, in 1804, the Lewis and Clark Expedition was tasked with the job of surveying the region and charting its rivers.

2   The mission was a success, but their land route would prove too difficult for wagons. The passes across the Rocky Mountains could be traveled only on foot, or on horseback. So, beginning in 1810, fur trappers and traders began carving a new trail out west. With the new trail, people could travel west faster by land routes.

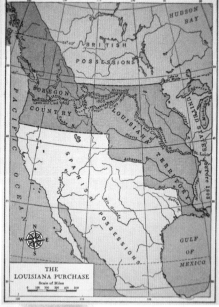

HISTORICAL PERSPECTIVE

In 1804, the Lewis and Clark Expedition set off from Missouri to explore the American West, accompanied by their guide and interpreter, Sacajawea. In a letter to Lewis and Clark, President Thomas Jefferson wrote the following instructions:

The object of your mission is to explore the Missouri river, & such principal stream of it, as, by its course & communication with the water of the Pacific Ocean may offer the most direct & practicable water communication across this continent, for the purposes of commerce.

The route West was first mapped by Lewis and Clark. The information they brought back helped map the future migration.

The Migration Begins

3   Of the lush green fields, abundant game, and the many rivers in the Louisiana Territory, William Clark wrote, "The Plains of this country are covered with a Leek Green Grass, well calculated for the sweetest and most nourishing hay . . . and nature appears to have exerted herself to beautify the scenery."

4   By the 1820s, land in the East was scarce, and what little was available for purchase was rocky and hard to farm. Word had spread that the land west of the Rocky Mountains in Oregon Territory was fertile and good for farming. Struggling farmers began to think about moving west, where the land was better and plentiful. So, the wave of settlers moving west began.

5   The people migrating west called themselves "emigrants" because they were leaving the states for unknown territories. Most of the people migrating kept diaries to record their journeys. One woman who wrote a daily account of her journey on the Oregon Trail was Narcissa Whitman.

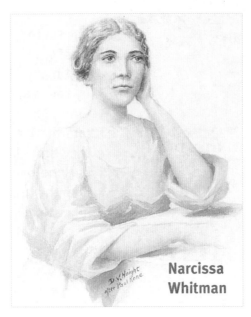

Narcissa Whitman

6   In 1836, Whitman and her husband, Marcus, led a small expedition from New York to Oregon to found a mission in Oregon Territory. She described their daily routines and mishaps in her diary and letters. She also wrote about the landscape, which was very different from New York, where she had lived. She described the landscape in a letter to her brother and sister on June 3, 1836:

7   "The face of the country yesterday afternoon and today has been rolling sand bluffs, mostly barren, quite unlike what our eyes have been satiated [filled] with for weeks past. No timber nearer than the Platte, and the water tonight is very bad—got from a small ravine."

8   Life on the trail was very different from life back East. Whitman writes, "Our fuel for cooking since we left timber . . . has been dried buffalo dung . . . similar to the kind of coal used in Pennsylvania."

Emigrants traveled in wagon trains along the trail.

Bison was a major source of food along the trail.

9   On the trail, travelers quickly recognized the importance of the American bison that roamed the plains. The men would hunt the buffalo for meat. Whitman recounts,

10   "The present time in our journey is a very important one. The hunter brought us buffalo meat yesterday for the first time. . . . We have some for supper tonight. . . . I expect it will be very good." However, the party had to eat buffalo meat so often that Whitman soon tired of it and longed for simple bread and butter. She writes that she has been "living on buffalo meat until I am cloyed [disgusted] with it."

11   Whitman and her party made it to Oregon. Upon reaching where they would settle and build their mission, she wrote, "You can better imagine our feelings this morning than we can describe them. I could not realize that the end of our long journey was so near." After traveling 3,200 kilometers (2,000 miles), the Whitmans had finally reached their new home in December 1836. Like many other emigrants, they were tired and weary, but happy and relieved to have made it.

Notes

This mural from the Oregon State Capitol shows Narcissa Whitman (left) greeting John McLoughlin, a prominent Oregon leader, after her journey west

12   The Whitmans settled in the eastern part of what is now the state of Washington. They built a mission there. Here Narcissa describes the new land and home:

13   "It is indeed, a lovely situation. We are on a beautiful level—a peninsula formed by the branches of the Walla Walla river, upon the base of which our house stands, on the southeast corner, near the shore of the main river. To run a fence across to the opposite river, on the north from our house—this, with the river, would enclose 300 acres of good land for cultivation, all directly under the eye. The rivers are barely skirted with timber. This is all the woodland we can see; beyond them, as far as the eye can reach, plains and mountains appear."

14   At first, the Whitmans worked well with the local Native Americans, the Cayuse. Over time, however, the differences between the two cultures grew. Tensions mounted when an outbreak of measles killed half the Cayuse tribe. Some Cayuse blamed the outbreak on Narcissa's husband, who was a doctor and whose medicine seemed to cure only white children.

The Migration Explodes

15   Soon after Narcissa Whitman made her trek on the Oregon Trail, others began to migrate there, too. In 1842, a party of more than 100 people set off. Soon the numbers increased dramatically. So many people began to venture west that the migration was called "Oregon Fever."

16   In 1843, around 1,000 men, women, and children left Elm Grove, Missouri, for the West. The emigrants formed a wagon train and embarked on the Oregon Trail. There were more than 100 covered wagons and a herd of about 5,000 oxen and cattle that set off on the 3,200-km (2,000-mile) journey. The travelers faced many hardships and dangers. Many believed Native American attacks posed the greatest threat, but crossing rivers was also treacherous, and the weather was unpredictable. Sudden downpours, snowstorms, and hailstorms could divert the wagon train. Wagons would break down. The journey could take up to six months, and disease spread quickly among the people. Still, they pressed on, hoping to reach Oregon safely and begin a new life there.

A wagon breaks down on the trail. This was a common hazard for migrants.

The Gold Rush

17   The migration on the Oregon Trail became an annual event. Thousands of emigrants began to join the wagon trains heading west. Then in 1848, gold was discovered in California. The lure of rich farmlands now changed to fields of gold. By

Gold brought many people west after 1848.

1850, more than 50,000 people traveled the Oregon Trail west. Instead of turning toward Oregon near the end of the trail, many turned to California. They hoped to find their fortune mining or panning for gold instead of farming.

The End of the Trail

18   By 1869, railroads connected California to the rest of the country and people moved west—using trains instead of wagons. The trail became a route for cattle drives, but by the 1900s most stopped using the trail and it became obsolete. With new means of transportation, it was no longer needed.

a wagon train heading west

19   However, many pioneers kept the tales of the Oregon Trail alive. In 1852, pioneer Ezra Meeker wrote *Ox-Team Days on the Oregon Trail,* a book about the many emigrants who traveled west to the trail's end:

Ezra Meeker on the trail

20   "At length, after we had endured five long months of soul-trying travel and had covered about eighteen hundred miles, counting from the crossing of the Missouri, we dragged ourselves on to the end. . . . The appearance of this crowd of emigrants beggars description. . . . Friendships, sincere and lasting, came as one of the sweet rewards of those days of common struggle and adversity." [from chapter 9]

21   Meeker worked to make the Oregon Trail a historic landmark, and today, it is. In 1978, Congress made it a historic trail. People can now follow the route of the Oregon Trail. And with the many diaries from the time, people can read what life on the Oregon Trail was like, too.

Today the Oregon Trail is a historic landmark.

Remember to annotate as you read.

Notes

Oregon Trail Diary

1   Dear Diary,

2   I know I've not written for several weeks, but for good reason. In early September, we crossed the Blue Mountains of Oregon, which proved to be the most difficult part of our journey thus far!

3   The mountains were very steep, so the trip was challenging, with many obstacles. There was snow in some places, making the crossing even harder. Pa and the other men tied ropes to the wagons and pulled them up the side of the mountains. We all had to walk, even the young children.

4   When the rope broke on the Smiths' wagon, we were terrified! We watched in horror as the wagon tumbled down the side of the mountain, but there was nothing to do but to continue walking. For two straight days it rained, and everyone was wet and cold. Finally, we made it to the other side of the mountain. Since the Smiths lost their supplies, the rest of us pitched in and helped them. We have become like one big family!

5   Next week, we'll cross the Columbia River, and if all goes well, we should reach Oregon City a few weeks later. Pa plans to buy 250 acres of land, and then we'll build our new home. I'm eager to live in a house again and sleep in a real bed! And I can start school again once we are settled. I can't wait!

6   Your friend Sally

September 17, 1845

BuildReflectWrite

Build Knowledge

In response to reading "The Oregon Trail," record your ideas in the chart below.

Oregon Trail
1. Identify some of the causes of the migration along the trail.
2. Describe the dangers and challenges emigrants faced on the trail.
3. Summarize what daily life was like for emigrants on the trail.

Reflect

How do communities evolve?

Based on this week's texts, write down new ideas and questions you have about the essential question.

_____

_____

_____

_____

_____

_____

Writing to Sources

Opinion

In this unit, you have learned about three pathways that connected communities across North America—the Oregon Trail, the transcontinental railroad, and Route 66. In your opinion, which of these pathways did the most to connect people and places? In a short essay, state and support your opinion on this topic, using evidence from three texts in this unit.

Support for Collaborative Conversation

Discussion Prompts

Express ideas or opinions . . .

When I read _____, it made me think that _____.

Based on the information in _____, my [opinion/idea] is _____.

As I [listened to/read/watched] _____, it occurred to me that _____.

It was important that_____.

Gain the floor . . .

I would like to add a comment. _____.

Excuse me for interrupting, but _____.

That made me think of _____.

Build on a peer's idea or opinion . . .

That's an interesting point. It makes me think _____.

If _____, then maybe _____.

[Name] said _____. That could mean that _____.

Express agreement with a peer's idea . . .

I agree that _____ because _____.

I also feel that _____ because _____.

[Name] made the comment that _____, and I think that is important because _____.

Respectfully express disagreement . . .

I understand your point of view that _____, but in my opinion _____ because _____.

That is an interesting idea, but did you consider the fact that _____?

I do not agree that _____. I think that _____ because _____.

Ask a clarifying question . . .

You said _____. Could you explain what you mean by that?

I don't understand how your evidence supports that inference. Can you say more?

I'm not sure I understand. Are you saying that _____?

Clarify for others . . .

When I said _____, what I meant was that _____.

I reached my conclusion because_____.

Group Roles

Discussion Director:
Your role is to guide the group's discussion and be sure that everyone has a chance to express his or her ideas.

Notetaker:
Your job is to record the group's ideas and important points of discussion.

Summarizer:
In this role, you will restate the group's comments and conclusions.

Presenter:
Your role is to provide an overview of the group's discussion to the class.

Timekeeper:
You will track the time and help to keep your peers on task.

Making Meaning with Words

Word	My Definition	My Sentence
affected (p. 12)		
appearance (p. 29)		
charting (p. 22)		
convinced (p. 15)		
expand (p. 13)		
extremely (p. 4)		
progress (p. 17)		
region (p. 6)		
surveying (p. 22)		
venture (p. 27)		

760L–1010L

Build Knowledge Across 10 Topic Strands

Government and Citizenship

Character

Life Science

Point of View

Technology and Society

Theme

History and Culture
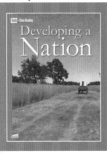

Earth Science
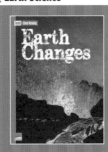

Economics
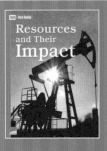

Physical Science
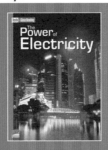

Benchmark
UNIVERSE.COM™
BENCHMARK EDUCATION COMPANY

Grade 4 • U

ISBN 978-1-490
9 781490 092034
Y16045

T3-AEM-488